YAKALOU MEDIA

GET CLARITY ABOUT YOUR WORK–LIFE BALANCE

100 Questions To Ask Yourself To Improve, Achieve And Maintain A Good Work–life Balance

Contents

Disclaimer   v

I   BEFORE EVERYTHING

Introduction   3
How This Book Can Help You   5
The 5 Rules To Get The Most Out Of This Book   7
Your Journey, Your Way   9

II   The 100 Questions To Ask Yourself To
Achieve And Maintain A Good Work-life Balance

Chapter 1: Self-Reflection and Goals   15
Exercise #1   18
Chapter 2: Time Management   19
Exercise #2   22
Chapter 3: Stress and Well-being   23
Exercise #3   26
Chapter 4: Career Satisfaction   27
Exercise #4   30
Chapter 5: Family and Relationships   31
Exercise #5   34
Chapter 6: Health and Fitness   35

Exercise #6   38

Chapter 7: Personal Growth and Hobbies   39

Exercise #7   42

Chapter 8: Financial Stability   43

Exercise #8   46

Chapter 9: Work Environment and Culture   47

Exercise #9   50

Chapter 10: Long-term Planning   51

Exercise #10   54

Conclusion   55

Disclaimer

This book is designed to provide information only. This information is provided and sold with the knowledge that the publisher and author do not offer any legal or other professional advice. In the case of a need for any such expertise, consult with the appropriate professional.

This book does not contain all the information available on the subject. This book has not been created to be specific to any individual's or organization's situation or needs. Every effort has been made to make this book as accurate as possible. However, there may be typographical and/or content errors. Therefore, this book should serve only as a general guide, not as the ultimate source of subject information.

This book contains information that might be dated and is intended only to educate and entertain. Regarding any loss or damage allegedly suffered or alleged to have occurred as a result of the information in this book, either directly or indirectly, the author and publisher shall have no liability or responsibility to any person or entity.

I

BEFORE EVERYTHING

Introduction

Have you ever felt like you're running on a treadmill that just won't stop? Where do the lines between your work hours and personal time seem to blur, leaving you exhausted yet unfulfilled? This is the reality for many in our fast-paced world, where the demands of our jobs often overshadow our personal lives. But what if you could hit the pause button, step back, and find harmony between your career and personal life? This is where the concept of work-life balance comes into play—a crucial equilibrium that is not just desirable but essential for our well-being and happiness.

Imagine a life where you have time for a fulfilling career but also for your family, hobbies, and self-care. It sounds ideal, doesn't it? This book is your guide to making that vision a reality. It is crafted to help you ask the right questions—the kind that encourages you to reflect deeply and honestly about how you manage your time, handle stress, and prioritize your goals. How often do you reflect on your daily routine, questioning if it aligns with your true aspirations? Do you ponder how your job affects your relationships, health, and inner peace? These are the types of questions that this book will help you explore.

Using this book is like having a conversation with a wise friend. It's not about giving you a one-size-fits-all solution, because everyone's ideal balance looks different. Instead, it's about guiding you to ask yourself the right questions—questions that lead to personalized, actionable insights. Each section of this book deals with a different aspect of your life, from your mental health to your relationships, from your career satisfaction to your long-term financial planning. By engaging with these sections, you will gradually uncover the unique blend of work and life that best suits you.

So, how do you begin? Start by reading through each section at your own pace. Reflect on each question and jot down your thoughts. Be honest with yourself; this book is a judgement-free zone. The journey to achieving a balanced life requires patience and self-awareness. Remember, this book is not a quick fix, but a companion on your journey to a more fulfilling life. As you turn these pages, you're taking the first step towards reclaiming your time, finding joy in both work and play, and ultimately crafting a life that you don't need a vacation from. Let's embark on this journey together, shall we?

How This Book Can Help You

Have you ever paused and wondered, "Is this the life I always wanted?" If you find yourself questioning the balance between your work commitments and the life you dream of outside the office, then this book is your beacon. Let's talk about how this book can be the catalyst for the change you've been longing for.

In the hustle of meeting deadlines and juggling responsibilities, it's easy to lose sight of what's truly important. This book is designed to be your guide to rediscovering and realigning your priorities. It doesn't just offer advice; it asks you the right questions—the kind that prompts you to reflect deeply and honestly about your current lifestyle. How often do you get the chance to pause and think about what makes you truly happy?

Each chapter in this book is structured to address different facets of your life, from managing stress at work to nurturing relationships at home. These aren't just chapters; they're stepping stones towards a more balanced and fulfilling life. Think of this book as a conversation with a friend who gently nudges you to look at your life from a fresh perspective.

But how exactly does this book help? It offers a mirror for self-reflection. As you progress through each chapter, you'll be encouraged to ask yourself questions you might have been avoiding. What are your true passions? Are you compromising your health for your job? How can you make more time for your loved ones? These questions are the keys to unlocking a more balanced and meaningful life.

Moreover, this book is a toolbox filled with practical strategies and tips. It doesn't just leave you with questions; it guides you towards solutions. You'll find methods to better manage your time, reduce stress, and make decisions that align with your personal values. The aim is to equip you with skills that transform how you approach work and life.

Lastly, this book is a journey of self-discovery. As you turn each page, you might find aspects of your life that you want to improve or change. Embrace these revelations. The realization is the first step towards transformation. Remember, achieving work-life balance is not a destination but a continuous journey of making choices that align with your ideal life.

So, are you ready to take this journey? Are you prepared to ask yourself some tough questions and make meaningful changes? This book is your companion, guiding you towards a life where work complements your personal happiness, not compromises it. Let's embark on this path together, towards a more balanced and fulfilling life.

The 5 Rules To Get The Most Out Of This Book

Welcome to the first step of your journey towards a balanced life. Before we dive into the heart of the matter, let's establish some ground rules. These rules aren't strict commands; think of them as friendly guidelines to help you navigate through this book effectively. They are designed to ensure that your journey through these pages is not just informative, but transformative.

Rule 1: Be Honest with Yourself

Ask yourself: When was the last time you were truly honest about your needs and desires? This book requires that level of honesty. As you explore the questions in each chapter, answer them sincerely. It's okay if some truths are uncomfortable; growth often starts there. Remember, this book is a safe space for self-reflection.

Rule 2: Take Your Time

Rome wasn't built in a day, and neither is a well-balanced life. Don't rush through the chapters. Take the time to digest each question and what it means for you. Let the ideas simmer in your mind. Maybe revisit a chapter after a day or two; you might find new insights with a fresh perspective.

Rule 3: Embrace the Process

Change is a process, not an event. As you work through this book, remember that small, consistent steps lead to significant changes. Some sections will challenge you more than others. Embrace these challenges as part of your growth journey.

Rule 4: Apply What You Learn

How often have you read something inspiring, only to forget it a few days later? To avoid this, apply the insights you gain immediately. Experiment with new ways to balance your work and personal life, even if they feel awkward at first. Real-life application is where the true magic happens.

Rule 5: Reflect and Revisit

Finally, make reflection a habit. After completing a chapter, take a moment to reflect on what you've learned. How does it apply to your life? What changes do you need to make? It's also beneficial to revisit chapters after some time. As you grow and your life evolves, you'll find new meanings in the same words.

By following these five simple rules, you'll be setting yourself up for a successful journey through this book and, more importantly, towards a life where work and personal satisfaction coexist harmoniously. Ready to turn the page? Let's start this journey with an open mind and a willing heart.

Your Journey, Your Way

Imagine you're on a road trip. You have your map, but you don't need to follow a predetermined path. You can choose to explore a side road that looks intriguing or pause at a scenic spot that catches your eye. This book is much like that road trip. While you can certainly read it from cover to cover, you don't have to. You have the freedom to skip around and dive into the sections that resonate with where you are in your life right now.

Perhaps today you're grappling with work-related stress, and you're looking for immediate relief. There's a chapter for that. Maybe tomorrow you'll be pondering over your personal relationships and seeking guidance on how to nurture them. There's a section for those thoughts as well. This book is designed to be versatile, to be your companion on whatever part of your journey you find yourself on at any given moment.

Let's say you're feeling overwhelmed by the demands of your job. You don't have to wade through chapters on financial planning or personal hobbies first. You can jump straight to the section about managing workplace stress. Here, you'll find questions and advice tailored to help you navigate these specific challenges. This targeted approach ensures that you get the support and guidance you need, exactly when you need it.

On the other hand, you might be in a place where your

career feels fulfilling, but you're struggling to find time for personal growth or hobbies. Why sift through pages about career satisfaction when you can go directly to the section on personal development? This book is structured to allow you to identify and focus on the areas of your life that need attention, without the need to follow a linear path.

This approach has a unique advantage. It acknowledges that your life is dynamic and that your needs can change from day to day. Today's pressing concern might be finding a better work-life balance, but in a week, you might need advice on setting long-term personal goals. By giving you the freedom to navigate the book as you please, it mirrors the fluidity of real life.

Moreover, this method can be incredibly empowering. It puts you in the driver's seat, allowing you to take control of your journey. You're not passively absorbing information; you're actively seeking out what's relevant to you. This active engagement can make the insights you gain all the more impactful. When you find a chapter or a question that resonates with you, it's because you've identified a current, relevant need in your life.

Remember, the goal of this book is not just to provide answers but to spark questions that lead to personal revelations and growth. Feel free to leaf through the pages, to pause where something piques your interest, or to skip sections until you find the one that speaks to your current situation. There's no right or wrong way to use this book. Like a trusty map, it's here to guide you, no matter which route you choose to take on your journey to a balanced and fulfilling life.

As you continue this journey, remember that every chapter and every question in this book is a potential tool for your growth and happiness. Use them as you see fit, and don't hesitate to revisit them as your life evolves. This book is not just a one-time read; it's a resource you can turn to again and again, whenever you need it.

II

The 100 Questions To Ask Yourself To Achieve And Maintain A Good Work-life Balance

Chapter 1: Self-Reflection and Goals

Meet Emily. Emily is a marketing executive in a bustling city. Every day, she finds herself swamped with meetings, emails, and deadlines. While she's excelling in her career, her personal life seems to be on hold. Her hobbies have become distant memories, and her social life is dwindling. It's during one particularly long night at the office that Emily realizes something needs to change. This story is not uncommon. Like Emily, many of us get so caught up in our work that we forget to live. This chapter is about finding Emily—the part of you that yearns for balance and fulfillment beyond work.

Self-reflection is the cornerstone of personal growth. It's about taking a step back and looking at your life with fresh eyes. Ask yourself: Are you like Emily, giving everything to your job but leaving little for yourself? Perhaps it's time to reassess your priorities. What do you value most in life? How much of your time and energy are you dedicating to these values?

Let's explore how to find a balance that works for you. Start by assessing your current work-life situation. Are you overworking to the point of exhaustion? Are you neglecting your health, your family, or your passions? These aren't just rhetorical questions; they're a wake-up call. A call to start setting personal and professional goals that align with what truly matters to you.

Setting goals is not just about career milestones or financial targets. It's about creating a vision for your life as a whole. What does your ideal day look like? How do you want to feel when you wake up in the morning? These goals are your roadmap to a more balanced and fulfilling life. Remember, goals are personal. They're not about what society expects of you, but about what you want for yourself.

Now, let's bring your focus to understanding your priorities. It's easy to say that family or health are your priorities, but do your daily actions reflect this? Sometimes, we need to make tough decisions to align our lives with our priorities. It might mean turning down a work project to attend your child's school play or choosing a healthy meal over a quick fast-food fix.

To help you on this journey of self-reflection and goal-setting, here are 10 questions to ponder and a practical exercise:

1. What are the three things you value most in life?
2. How does your current job align with these values?
3. What aspects of your work make you feel fulfilled?
4. Are there parts of your job that consistently cause stress?
5. How much quality time do you spend with loved ones each week?
6. What hobbies or passions have you neglected?
7. What does your ideal workday look like?
8. What changes can you make to your current routine to align more closely with your ideal day?
9. What are three personal goals you want to achieve in the next year?
10. What are three professional goals you want to achieve in the next year?

By engaging in self-reflection and setting clear goals, you're not just dreaming about a better life; you're taking the first steps towards making it a reality. Remember, like Emily, you have the power to change your story. Your journey to a balanced life starts now.

Exercise #1

Practical Exercise:

Create a "My Ideal Day" collage. Use images and words from magazines or printouts that represent what your perfect day would involve. Place it somewhere; you'll see it every day as a reminder of what you're working towards.

Chapter 2: Time Management

Let's consider the story of Alex, a project manager and father of two. Alex's days are a whirlwind of work tasks, family responsibilities, and an ever-growing to-do list. He often feels like he's running a never-ending race against time. One evening, while working late again, Alex wonders, "Is there a better way to manage all this?" This moment of reflection marks the beginning of his journey towards effective time management, a journey that many of us need to embark on.

Time management is more than just organizing your daily schedule. It's about making conscious decisions on how to efficiently use your time and balancing your professional responsibilities with personal happiness. For Alex and for many of us, mastering this balance is the key to a fulfilling life. Ask yourself: How often do you end your day feeling satisfied with how you spent your time? Are you constantly busy but not productive?

Evaluating how you use your time is a crucial first step. Take a moment to think about your typical day. How much of your time is spent on work, and how much is left for your family, hobbies, and rest? This isn't about judging yourself; it's about gaining clarity. Recognizing where your time goes is the first step to taking control of your schedule.

Now, let's talk about strategies for effective time allocation. It's not just about doing more in less time; it's about doing what's important. For Alex, it meant learning to say no to less critical tasks at work and delegating where possible. At home, it involved creating a shared family calendar to keep track of everyone's activities. What strategies could work for you? Could it be setting specific work hours or perhaps planning your week every Sunday evening?

Prioritizing tasks is an art. It's about distinguishing between what's urgent and what's important. Often, we get caught up in the urgency of certain tasks, losing sight of what truly matters. A useful tip is to categorize tasks into four quadrants: urgent and important, important but not urgent, urgent but not important, and neither urgent nor important. This method can help you focus on tasks that align with your long-term goals and values.

To assist you in mastering time management, here are 10 thought-provoking questions and a practical exercise:

1. How do you currently manage your daily schedule?
2. What are the most time-consuming tasks in your day?
3. Which tasks bring you the most satisfaction?
4. Are there activities you can delegate or eliminate?
5. How much time do you allocate to self-care and relaxation?
6. What changes can you make to reduce time spent on unproductive activities?
7. How can you better organize your tasks at work and at home?
8. What tools or methods could help you manage your time more effectively?
9. How do you handle interruptions and distractions?
10. What does a balanced and well-managed day look like for

you?

Remember, like Alex, you have the power to transform how you use your time. Effective time management is not just about being efficient; it's about creating a life where your time reflects your values and brings you joy. Let's take control of our time and, in turn, take control of our lives.

Exercise #2

Practical Exercise:

For one week, keep a time diary. Record how you spend each hour of your day, from work tasks to leisure activities. At the end of the week, review this diary to identify patterns and areas for improvement.

Chapter 3: Stress and Well-being

Meet Sara, a dedicated nurse who often finds herself over-whelmed by the demands of her job. She loves helping others, but the long hours and high-stress environment have begun to take a toll on her well-being. One quiet evening, sitting in her garden, Sara realizes that to take care of others, she first needs to take care of herself. Her story highlights a common struggle many face: managing stress without compromising our well-being.

Understanding stress in the workplace is crucial. It's not about eliminating stress completely; that's nearly impossible. Instead, it's about recognizing when it becomes harmful. Stress, when left unchecked, can lead to burnout, affecting both your professional and personal lives. Ask yourself, like Sara did, are there moments in your job that feel overwhelmingly stressful? What triggers these feelings?

The next step is identifying your stressors. This can be challenging, as stress often feels like a normal part of life. However, by pinpointing what causes your stress, you can start to find ways to manage it. Think about the factors in your work that contribute to your stress levels. Is it a particular task, a certain time of day, or maybe the environment itself?

Methods for stress management vary from person to person.

For Sara, it involved setting boundaries at work, practicing mindfulness, and finding time for activities she enjoyed. What methods could work for you? Sometimes, it's about saying no to extra responsibilities, or maybe it's finding a hobby that helps you unwind. Remember, managing stress is not a one-size-fits-all solution; it's about finding what resonates with you.

The importance of mental and emotional well-being cannot be overstated. When you're mentally and emotionally healthy, you're better equipped to face the challenges of your job and enjoy your personal life. Well-being is not just the absence of stress; it's about feeling fulfilled, balanced, and happy. How often do you check in with yourself to assess your mental and emotional state?

To guide you in managing stress and enhancing your well-being, here are 10 questions and a practical exercise:

1. What aspects of your job cause you the most stress?
2. How does stress manifest in your life (e.g., physical symptoms, mood changes)?
3. What are your current methods for dealing with stress?
4. How effective are these methods in reducing your stress levels?
5. What activities help you feel relaxed and rejuvenated?
6. How do you balance your professional and personal lives?
7. What steps can you take to create a more positive work environment?
8. How often do you take breaks during your workday?
9. In what ways can you improve your work-life balance to reduce stress?
10. What are your go-to strategies for maintaining mental and emotional well-being?

Like Sara, you have the power to change how stress affects your life. By understanding and managing stress, you can improve not only your performance at work but also the quality of your life outside of it. Let's embark on this journey of stress management together, towards a state of well-being and contentment.

Exercise #3

Practical Exercise:

Create a "Stress Management Plan." Write down your main stressors and develop a strategy for each to mitigate or cope with the stress. Include activities for relaxation and self-care.

Chapter 4: Career Satisfaction

Consider the story of David, a seasoned graphic designer at a large agency. For years, he's poured his heart into his work, but lately, he's been feeling a sense of unfulfillment. His job, once a source of joy, now feels like a routine task. One lazy Sunday afternoon, while sketching in his backyard, David ponders over his career path. It's at this moment of introspection that he decides to reassess his job satisfaction and realign his career with his passions and values. David's journey mirrors a question many professionals face: How can I find fulfillment in my career?

Assessing job satisfaction is the first step. It's easy to get caught up in the daily grind and lose sight of what you initially loved about your job. Like David, ask yourself, What drew you to your current profession? Does your job still give you that same sense of excitement and satisfaction? Understanding what you value in your work is crucial to gauging your job satisfaction.

Reflecting on career fulfillment goes beyond evaluating your current job. It's about looking at your career as a whole. What are your aspirations? Do you see a path forward in your current role? Career fulfillment often comes from a sense of progress and growth. Think about how your current job aligns with your long-term career goals.

Aligning career goals with personal life is vital for overall satisfaction. A fulfilling career should complement, not compromise, your personal life. For David, this meant considering how his job affected his time with family and his personal hobbies. How does your job fit into the larger picture of your life? Are your career choices helping you lead the life you want?

Making career choices that enhance work-life balance is the ultimate goal. Sometimes, this might mean seeking new opportunities or even a career change. Other times, it could be as simple as setting boundaries or negotiating for flexibility. The key is to make conscious choices that bring you closer to the balance you seek.

To help you navigate the path to career satisfaction, here are 10 questions and a practical exercise:

1. What aspects of your current job do you enjoy the most?
2. Are there parts of your job that you find unfulfilling or draining?
3. How does your job align with your personal values and passions?
4. What are your long-term career aspirations?
5. How does your current job contribute to your overall life satisfaction?
6. Are there opportunities for growth and development in your current role?
7. How does your work-life balance currently look?
8. What changes can you make in your current role to improve satisfaction?
9. Are you willing to explore new opportunities or a career change for more fulfillment?
10. How can you align your career goals with your personal

life?

David's story is a testament to the fact that reassessing and realigning your career is not just possible but necessary for your overall happiness. Whether you're just starting in your profession or are well into your career, it's never too late to seek career satisfaction. Let's take the first step towards a career that not only meets our professional aspirations but also enriches our personal lives.

Exercise #4

Practical Exercise:

Create a "Career Vision Board." Include images and words that represent your ideal career and the balance you seek with your personal life. Place it where you can see it daily as a visual reminder of your career aspirations.

Chapter 5: Family and Relationships

Meet Lisa, a busy software developer and a mother of two. Her life is a balancing act between demanding work projects and her role as a parent and spouse. Recently, she's noticed her work commitments spilling over into family time, often missing dinners and her children's school events. One evening, her daughter asks, "Mom, why are you always working?" This simple question hits Lisa hard, sparking a realization about the impact of her work on her family and relationships.

Understanding the impact of work on family and relationships is crucial. In today's fast-paced world, it's easy to let work consume us, often at the expense of personal relationships. Like Lisa, take a moment to reflect—has your work life encroached upon your family time? Are your relationships suffering because of your work commitments? Acknowledging the effect of your professional life on your personal one is the first step toward change.

Gauging work's effect on personal relationships involves honest self-assessment. How often do you bring work stress home? Are you mentally present during family interactions, or are you distracted by work thoughts? These questions aren't meant to induce guilt but to foster awareness. By understanding how your work affects your relationships, you can start to make the necessary adjustments.

Balancing family time with work commitments is a delicate art. It requires setting clear boundaries between work and personal life. Consider your current work-life balance—are you able to switch off from work during family time? Lisa started by designating 'family hours' where work discussions or emails were off-limits. Think about the changes you can implement to ensure quality time with your loved ones.

Strategies for family inclusion and communication are essential. It's about creating an environment where every family member feels valued and heard. This might mean having regular family meetings to discuss schedules, challenges, and fun activities. Open communication is key. Involve your family in discussions about your work schedule, listen to their concerns, and together find solutions that work for everyone.

To help you strengthen your family and personal relationships, here are 10 questions and a practical exercise:

1. How often does your work interfere with your family time?
2. Are you able to disconnect from work during family activities?
3. How does your work schedule affect your relationships with your partner and children?
4. What can you do to be more present during family interactions?
5. How often do you talk with your family about your work commitments?
6. Are there ways you can involve your family in your work life without overwhelming them?
7. How can you make your family feel valued despite your busy schedule?

8. What changes can you make to ensure quality family time?
9. How can you improve communication with your family about work-related stress?
10. What family activities can you plan to strengthen your relationships?

Lisa's story is a reminder that balancing work and family is not only about time management but also about emotional presence and open communication. As we navigate our professional lives, let's not forget the ones who support us through it all. Strengthening our family bonds and personal relationships is key to a fulfilling life. Let's make our loved ones a priority, not an afterthought.

Exercise #5

Practical Exercise:

Plan a 'Family Board Meeting.' Once a week, sit down with your family to discuss the week ahead. Talk about everyone's schedules, plan family activities, and address any concerns. This regular check-in ensures everyone feels included and respected.

Chapter 6: Health and Fitness

Consider the story of Kevin, an IT consultant whose life revolves around tight deadlines and long hours in front of a computer. Fast food and little physical activity have gradually replaced his once active lifestyle. Lately, Kevin has noticed a decline in his energy levels and motivation, affecting both his work and personal life. It's during a particularly sluggish morning, struggling to focus on a report, that Kevin realizes the critical role of health and fitness in maintaining work-life balance.

The role of physical health in work-life balance is often underestimated. We sometimes forget that our physical well-being directly impacts our efficiency, mood, and overall quality of life. Like Kevin, ask yourself: Are you taking care of your body? How often do you prioritize exercise and proper nutrition in your busy schedule? Acknowledging the importance of health is the first step towards a balanced and productive life.

Assessing health and fitness routines is essential. Take a moment to reflect on your daily habits. How much physical activity do you get? What does your diet look like? Are you getting enough sleep? These aren't just routine questions; they're a self-check on how you are treating your body amidst the demands of work.

Incorporating exercise and healthy habits into our lives can seem daunting, especially with a demanding job. However, it's about finding small, sustainable changes that can fit into your routine. For Kevin, this meant starting with short, daily walks and gradually incorporating more activities into his weekends. Consider your schedule and think about where you can make room for health and fitness. Remember, even small changes can lead to significant improvements in your overall well-being.

Balancing your work schedule with your health goals is about creating a harmonious routine. It's not about choosing work over health or vice versa; it's about integrating both into your life. This might involve setting specific times for workouts, preparing healthy meals in advance, or ensuring you get enough sleep each night. The key is to view health as a non-negotiable aspect of your life, just like your work commitments.

To help you prioritize your health and fitness, here are 10 questions and a practical exercise:

1. How often do you engage in physical activity?
2. What types of physical activities do you enjoy?
3. How does your current diet affect your energy levels and work performance?
4. Are there any unhealthy habits you would like to change?
5. How many hours of sleep do you get on average, and how does it affect your day?
6. How can you incorporate more physical activity into your daily routine?
7. What changes can you make to your diet for better health?
8. How can you ensure a balance between work commitments and health goals?
9. What are your specific health and fitness goals?
10. How can you make health and fitness a priority despite a

busy work schedule?

Kevin's story is a reminder that health and fitness are not just about looking good; they are about feeling good and performing at our best in every aspect of life. By taking care of our physical well-being, we set ourselves up for success both in our professional and personal lives. Let's commit to making health a priority, not an afterthought in our busy lives.

Exercise #6

Practical Exercise:

Create a 'Health and Fitness Plan.' Outline specific, achievable goals for your physical activity and diet. Schedule regular check-ins to track your progress and adjust your plan as needed.

Chapter 7: Personal Growth and Hobbies

Meet Angela, a corporate lawyer who has always been deeply invested in her career. Her days are filled with client meetings, case studies, and court appearances. However, recently, Angela has begun to feel a certain emptiness. One quiet Saturday, she comes across an old guitar in her attic, a reminder of her once-loved hobby. Strumming a few chords, she feels a spark of joy, long forgotten in the hustle of her career. This moment marks a turning point for Angela, as she realizes the importance of personal interests and hobbies outside of her work.

The importance of personal interests outside of work cannot be overstated. In a world where professional success often takes center stage, hobbies and personal interests provide a necessary balance. They are not just leisure activities; they are vital for our mental and emotional health. Ask yourself, like Angela, have you set aside time for hobbies or interests that bring you joy?

Exploring hobbies and passions is a journey of self-discovery. It's about reconnecting with the things that you love that make you who you are beyond your professional identity. What activities excite you or pique your curiosity? Have you always wanted to learn a new skill or revisit an old hobby? These questions are invitations to explore and embrace your passions.

Making time for personal development is essential in our busy lives. It's easy to say there's no time for hobbies, but it's about making time. This could mean scheduling an hour a week for painting, joining a weekend book club, or taking an online course in something you've always been interested in. It's about prioritizing yourself and your interests as much as you do your work.

The benefits of diverse interests for overall well-being are numerous. Engaging in hobbies has been linked to reduced stress, increased creativity, and a greater sense of fulfillment. For Angela, playing the guitar became a way to unwind and express herself. It offered a balance in her life, enhancing her well-being and even positively impacting her work performance. Diverse interests bring a richness to our lives that work alone cannot provide.

To encourage your journey in personal growth and hobbies, here are 10 questions and a practical exercise:

1. What hobbies or activities did you enjoy in the past?
2. Are there any new interests you would like to explore?
3. How do your hobbies and interests reflect your personality and values?
4. How much time do you currently dedicate to personal interests outside of work?
5. What are the barriers that prevent you from pursuing your hobbies?
6. How can you integrate your interests into your regular schedule?
7. What resources or support do you need to pursue your hobbies?
8. How do your hobbies and interests contribute to your sense

of well-being?

9. In what ways can your hobbies enrich your personal and professional lives?

10. What steps can you take today to reconnect with or discover new hobbies?

Angela's rediscovery of her love for music is a beautiful reminder of how hobbies and personal interests can rejuvenate and enrich our lives. They offer an escape, a way to recharge, and an opportunity to grow outside our professional roles. Let's take the time to cultivate our interests, recognizing that in doing so, we are nurturing an integral part of our well-being and identity.

Exercise #7

Practical Exercise:

Create a 'Hobby Action Plan.' List down three hobbies or interests you want to pursue. For each, set specific, achievable goals, and plan how and when you will engage in these activities.

Chapter 8: Financial Stability

Let's delve into the life of Thomas, an architect who enjoys his work but often finds himself worrying about finances. Despite a good income, constant stress about savings, investments, and future financial security looms over him. He dreams of traveling and spending more time with his family but feels chained to his desk to meet his financial obligations. It's during a particularly stressful month-end budgeting session that Thomas realizes the need for a better financial plan to achieve the work-life balance he desires.

Financial planning is crucial for a balanced life. It's not just about earning well; it's about managing your finances to support the life you want to lead. Like Thomas, many of us face financial stress, not because we aren't earning enough but because we lack a clear financial plan. How often do you review your financial situation? Are your financial decisions aligned with your life goals?

Understanding your financial goals is the first step. What are you saving for? Is it retirement, your children's education, a dream vacation, or all of these? Setting clear financial goals can help you prioritize your spending and savings. It also provides a sense of direction and purpose for your financial decisions. Reflect on what financial security means to you and what goals you need to set to achieve it.

Balancing career choices and financial needs is a delicate act. It's about making career decisions that not only advance your professional aspirations but also support your financial goals. This might mean choosing a job with a better salary, even if it's more demanding, or opting for a less stressful job that pays less but gives you more time for personal pursuits. Consider, like Thomas, what trade-offs you're willing to make for financial stability and peace of mind.

Tips for financial management and stability can range from budgeting and saving to investing wisely. It's important to educate yourself on financial matters. Simple changes like tracking expenses, setting a budget, and planning for emergencies can significantly improve your financial health. Remember, financial stability isn't achieved overnight; it's a result of consistent and informed financial decisions over time.

To assist you in achieving financial stability, here are 10 questions and a practical exercise:

1. What are your short-term and long-term financial goals?
2. How well do you understand your current financial situation?
3. Are your spending habits aligned with your financial goals?
4. How much of your income are you saving regularly?
5. What financial knowledge do you need to improve upon (investing, budgeting, etc.)?
6. How does your career choice impact your financial stability?
7. What steps can you take to reduce unnecessary expenses?
8. How prepared are you for financial emergencies or unexpected events?

9. What are some ways you can increase your income or savings?
10. How can you make your money work for you through investments or other means?

Thomas's journey toward financial planning is a powerful reminder of how managing our finances effectively can lead to greater freedom and satisfaction in both our professional and personal lives. By taking control of our financial health, we open the door to more choices and opportunities, bringing us closer to the work-life balance we all strive for.

Exercise #8

Practical Exercise:

Develop a 'Personal Financial Plan.' List your financial goals, create a budget, plan for savings and investments, and consider insurance or emergency funds. Regularly review and adjust this plan to stay on track with your financial objectives.

Chapter 9: Work Environment and Culture

Meet Maya, a creative director at a bustling advertising agency. While she thrives in her role, she often finds herself drained by the high-pressure and competitive atmosphere of her workplace. Lately, she's begun to feel that the environment is stifling her creativity rather than nurturing it. As she sits in a café on a Sunday, sipping her coffee and observing the relaxed patrons, Maya contemplates the stark contrast to her work environment. This moment of clarity makes her realize the profound impact her workplace culture has on her life and well-being.

Examining your work environment is a critical step towards understanding its influence on your life. The environment in which you spend a significant portion of your day can greatly affect your mood, stress levels, and overall happiness. Think about your workplace: Is it supportive and collaborative, or competitive and high-pressure? Does it align with your values and work style? Like Maya, evaluate whether your work environment enhances or hinders your well-being.

Reflecting on workplace culture can provide insight into your job satisfaction and engagement. A positive culture can boost your motivation and productivity, while a negative one can lead to burnout and dissatisfaction. Consider the dynamics with your colleagues, the leadership style of your superiors, and the general ethos of the company. How do these factors affect your attitude towards work?

The impact of the work environment on personal life can be significant. A stressful or toxic work culture can seep into your personal time, affecting relationships, health, and leisure activities. Conversely, a supportive work environment can enhance your personal life, providing a sense of fulfillment and balance. Assess how your work environment influences your life outside of work. Are you able to switch off and relax, or does work-related stress follow you home?

Seeking support and changes at work is often necessary to improve your work-life balance and well-being. This might involve having open conversations with your manager about workload, seeking out a mentor for guidance, or even considering a change in your work setting or role. Think about the changes that could make your work life more rewarding and less stressful.

To help you navigate your work environment and culture, here are 10 questions and a practical exercise:

1. How would you describe the culture of your workplace?
2. Does your work environment align with your personal values and work style?
3. How do your interactions with colleagues and superiors affect your work experience?
4. Are you able to maintain a healthy work-life balance with your current work culture?
5. How does the stress level in your workplace impact your personal life?
6. What aspects of your work environment would you like to

change?

7. How supportive is your workplace in terms of personal development and well-being?
8. What steps can you take to improve your experience in your work environment?
9. Have you considered seeking a different work environment that better suits your needs?
10. What strategies can you employ to cope with challenges in your current work culture?

Maya's realization about her work environment is a journey many of us need to undertake. Our work culture plays a crucial role in our overall happiness and life satisfaction. By actively examining and addressing the aspects of our work environment that affect us, we can take steps towards a more fulfilling and balanced professional life.

Exercise #9

Practical Exercise:

Conduct a 'Work Environment Assessment.' For one week, note down observations about your workplace culture, interactions, and how they affect your mood and productivity. Use this assessment to identify areas for improvement or change.

Chapter 10: Long-term Planning

Meet Jordan, a seasoned marketing manager in his mid-forties. He's reached a comfortable stage in his career but often finds himself pondering about the future. He thinks about his aspirations when he first started his career and wonders if he's on the right path to achieving them. It's during a family vacation, while watching the sunset, that Jordan begins to map out his vision for the future. His story reflects a common realization many face as they navigate their career and life: the importance of long-term planning.

Creating a vision for the future is the first step in long-term planning. It involves looking beyond your current situation and imagining where you want to be in the years to come. What are your aspirations for your career and personal life? Like Jordan, take some time to dream about your ideal future without limitations. This vision will guide your decisions and actions moving forward.

Questions for long-term life and career planning are essential in shaping your path. Where do you see yourself in five, ten, or twenty years? What are the milestones you want to achieve? Consider your career trajectory, personal development, family life, and other aspects that are important to you. Reflecting on these questions can help clarify your long-term goals and the steps needed to achieve them.

Aligning your current balance with your future aspirations is crucial. It involves assessing your current lifestyle and work habits and determining if they align with your long-term goals. Are the choices you're making today helping you move closer to your vision for the future? For Jordan, this meant reevaluating his work-life balance and making changes that aligned with his future goals, such as pursuing further education and spending more quality time with his family.

Preparing for changes and transitions is part of long-term planning. Life is dynamic, and your plans may need to adapt to unexpected circumstances or new opportunities. How flexible are you in the face of change? What strategies can you develop to navigate future transitions smoothly? Anticipating and preparing for potential changes can make your journey towards your long-term goals more resilient and adaptable.

To assist you in your long-term planning, here are 10 questions and a practical exercise:

1. What does your ideal professional and personal life look like in the future?
2. What are your key long-term career goals?
3. How do your current work habits align with these long-term objectives?
4. What skills or knowledge do you need to acquire for your future aspirations?
5. How does your current lifestyle support or hinder your long-term goals?
6. What financial plans do you need to put in place for your future?
7. Are there any personal development goals you wish to

achieve?

8. How will you balance future family responsibilities with your career?
9. What contingency plans can you develop for unexpected life changes?
10. How often do you review and adjust your long-term plans?

Jordan's journey towards crafting his future vision illustrates the power of long-term planning. By taking the time to envision our future and align our current actions with these aspirations, we pave the way for a fulfilling and purposeful life. Let's embrace the process of planning for our future, preparing for its uncertainties, and celebrating its possibilities.

Exercise #10

Practical Exercise:

Draft a 'Future Roadmap.' Create a timeline for the next 5 to 20 years, mapping out key personal and professional milestones you aim to achieve. Regularly update this roadmap as your goals and circumstances evolve.

Conclusion

As we close the final chapter of this journey, I want to express my deepest gratitude to you for choosing and reading this book. By engaging with each chapter, you've taken significant steps towards understanding and achieving a harmonious work-life balance. Your commitment to personal growth and balance is not just inspiring; it's a testament to your dedication to living a fuller, more satisfying life.

In these pages, we've explored various facets of life, from managing time and stress to nurturing family relationships and personal health. We've delved into the importance of financial stability, a supportive work environment, and the joy of hobbies and personal interests. Each chapter was designed not just to provide insights but to encourage action and reflection.

As you continue on your path, remember that achieving and maintaining a balanced life is an ongoing process. It's about making conscious choices every day, aligning your actions with your values, and being adaptable to life's ever-changing circumstances. The journey towards balance is as unique as you are, and I hope this book has been a valuable companion along the way.

Now, I invite you to share your experience. Your review of this book can be incredibly powerful. Not only does it provide me with essential feedback, but it also helps other readers discover and benefit from these messages. Your insights and reflections could be the very thing someone else needs to hear to start their own journey towards a better work-life balance. By leaving a review, you're not just supporting me as an author; you're extending a hand to others who are seeking guidance and inspiration.

So, if you found value in these pages, please take a moment to share your thoughts and experiences. Your review could make a world of difference, helping to spread a message that has the power to transform lives.

In closing, thank you once again for embarking on this journey with me. May the path ahead be fulfilling, balanced, and enriched with the wisdom you've gathered here. Here's to a life well lived, in harmony with both our professional aspirations and our personal dreams.